Reveilles

NATHAN HOKS has published poems and translations in *Lit, Verse, Crazyhorse, Circumference*, and many other journals. He is the author of the chapbook *Birds Mistaken as Wind* (Rhyming Orange Press), and the translator of *Arctic Poems*, a collection of Vicente Huidobro's poetry forthcoming from Toad Press. A graduate of the Iowa Writers' Workshop, he lives in Somerville, Massachusetts.

Reveilles

Nathan Hoks

SALT

LONDON

PUBLISHED BY SALT PUBLISHING
Dutch House, 307–308 High Holborn, London wc1v 7LL United Kingdom

© Nathan Hoks, 2010

The right of Nathan Hoks to be identified as the
author of this work has been asserted by him in accordance
with Section 77 of the Copyright, Designs and Patents Act 1988.

Salt Publishing 2010

Printed and bound in the United States by Lightning Source Inc

Typeset in Swift 9.5 / 13

ISBN 978 1 84471 792 7 paperback

1 3 5 7 9 8 6 4 2

for Nikki

dozing off

Contents

Acknowledgements

Thank you to the editors of the following journals and anthologies in which some of these poems have appeared, often in slightly different versions: *Bateau, The Burnside Review, The Columbia Poetry Review, Court Green, Crazyhorse, CutBank, Dorado, Edna, Eye-Rhyme, GutCult, InDigest, Lungfull!, Mrs. Maybe, Octopus Magazine, Pilot Magazine,* and *Spinning Jenny*.

"The Cicatrix" first appeared in the chapbook *Birds Mistaken as Wind* (Rhyming Orange Press, 2003). "Coda" was printed on a broadside by Scott Sell in November, 2008.

Thank you to the Vermont Studio Center and the Millay Colony for the Arts for residencies during which some of these poems were written.

For their support, feedback and encouragement, thanks and love to Nikki, Chris, James, Joe, Jorge, Chad, Vieve, Kristin, Jared, Kate, Sarah, Scott, Dean, & my family.

Points

Behind the wall resides another wall
and behind that wall I'm not allowed
to look but yesterday you seemed
to emerge from behind no wall and I said
Wow, this is really teaching me a lesson
about walls. You appeared and we
ate pizza and when this was done the sun
had hardly started setting so we walked
through layers of bugs to the river which,
thank god, was still full of water holding
the moon's image between slim ripples.
Everything had leaves. We were impatient
to live. Okay, we said, we're not afraid
of cast iron falling on our heads, but behind
these words were a million other words,
words I have never heard, words you are
unhappy to hear, words I sometimes say
when alone rowing with a telephone.
I'm hungry, I said, let's move on, I'm tired
of talking about movies I haven't seen.
I never wish to dwell on details, not behind
the wall which holds back oceans of little walls.
When one spills out it's like a wave approaching.
Some try to stand on top and have a look
around. Some let it break across the face. I write
a poem called "Dew drops dew drops dew drops"
then cross the words out one by one.

Inside the Body

Saying things can be hard. I try
to keep quiet, but the apartment
does not clean itself. I fiasco with the
windstorm named after a young
woman I once knew in Chicago.
I hope her hair has grown back.
I hope her nose has stopped glowing.
I step onto the bus and walk
into a sudden recollection. I am
standing on my hands under-
water wondering why you are not
impressed. The new mangoes lie
in the fruit basket. Wow, that's
nearly perfect, and when I hold
the basket between my lips it is
an emblem of love. If I reach out
with my left hand it is to sell fish
wholesale. The right hand belches
and obeys nothing. These frantic
messengers with long hair and golden
belt buckles arrive calling for the
marriage of opposites. They are covered
in sweat and swearing at me. Why should
I show them my I.D? It's true, I delay
the obvious. All things made flesh
fall to pieces. For this we learn to speak.

Primer

1

I am tired of the unity of the chestnut tree.

2

The corrections come in the mail
and we turn them into paper airplanes.

3

We are trying to avoid ourselves.

4

We are a unity of limbs and words.

5

An arm bends. A toe dips into the mud.

6

The sky dribbles on the rooftops.

7

The salt shall leave the body.

Bread without Crust

Whenever I see myself
running toward myself
it is myself I am mostly

afraid of but also gray
matter, the grime inside
soap dishes, pencil

shavings (where do
they go?), dead or dying
flowers. The petals drop,

the stalks droop, the loops
are nothing new just as
the new is nothing

if not a label for soap
boxes. All the walkers walk
in circles, such is the

downward stream of most
beings, rooted or up-.

Navigator

1

Tour of the apricots.
Planet of the lemon drops.
Beachhead of the marble blocks.
Pasture of the pasture.

2

Helmet of the potato salad.
Cantor of the stimulus.
Cantor of the scratch and sniff.
Cantor of the ham & cheese.

3

I want a new fish.
I love the old fish.
Ocean of poster boys.
Ocean of poster boys.

4

Hill climb of the eye wear.
Hailstorm of the emperor.
Palace of the furniture sale.
Sofa of the empress.

5

Mountain of the firewheel.
Mouth of the lip balm.
Mouth of the picture show.
Mouth of the icecap.

Islands

The weeping crane does not fly forward.
The listless oboist has no note for green.

The pixilated beautician touches
her solvent to rejuvenate the nerve center.

The origami master lifts his wide-brimmed hat
to the lamp. He is calling up the sunbow.

One cannot ruin flowers, only floral arrangements.

Transmissions

Help, I'm a vortex, says the father
to the son who is weeping
behind the mud-covered windshield
as a stream of white cars flows by.
On the sidewalk a pigeon pauses
before crossing the pine's staggering shadow.
My, how you are useless, says
yellow to red, red pissing on daisies,
yellow clogging trash cans
in the back alley. The street lamp
can't wait to obliterate the shadows.
Water and sky move closer together.
Finches when I close my eyes.
Finches when changing light bulbs.
In the afternoon they sing underwater,
in the evening their songs are gusts,
throbbing voices: one finch
confuses itself with wind: it is nothing
but wings. I am not your father
but authority hereby forbids: Little Fucker,
close your eyes when you pray.

Greeting the Severed Music

The hilarious glass lady at the catfish
restaurant unbuttoned her blouse
and radiant cones of light emerged
dousing the whole room in this
white glow so it was impossible
to stay in the corner and snicker
as we had planned. We were looking
for the underground city which was
supposed to be somewhere between
the cathedral and the college, but
we confused the college for a museum
so when we were walking east
we were actually walking north
and by that time I was so hungry
it didn't really matter which sights we saw.
You held my hand and I could see
victory in your eyes. Happy, bleating
victory among lunch and drinks,
among fountains and clouds. You seemed
made of blue. I reached out
like a torch to a wasp's nest. The azaleas
and their bright shadows were flooding
the nearby garden. From this angle
the sky was like a mother and the frost
on the leaves was frost on the leaves.

Fuck the Cookies

I stand in the kitchen and
pretend I am baking though

I am mostly looking out
the window at the icicles
about to plunge to earth.

To be an icicle, I think, is
to live a singular destiny

in slow motion. Where
are the cookies? asks my

wife—oh, the cookies,
fuck the cookies, I say, and

we wash the empty plates
and dry the empty glasses.

Buffer Zones

Walkers walk by eyeing my cold
coffee as if to ask what do you think
of the lyric inventions of
the seventeenth century but I
don't think about the seventeenth
century, I am distracted by the train
whistle and the road construction
in the distance which seems further away
because of the breeze and leaves
and sunlight piling up like a giant
trash heap of sensations. Even if
you could stand on top of it you wouldn't
be able to track out this space.
The limits clash together. Car doors
are slamming and the slamming
is like an alarm clock calling you back
from a dream to which you were
indifferent. The black pavement
glistens. I guess it's wet though I don't
remember rain. The sunlight seems
to create small spots on my forehead.
When I furrow my brow, they expand
like ripples crossing the surface of
a calm lake. I wish I could step outside
and see them. I wish I were only ripples.
Like postmen they move around a lot
and end up going absolutely nowhere.

Light Air

I have broken various bones, femurs
included. People say I am falling
to pieces but I'm just looking for water,
in love with mindless motions of hand
and foot. Otherwise I am cautious.
I look both ways one to three times
before crossing the street. I bow
to the candle before going to bed.
Touch the boughs, prune the berries.
Push the butt and rub under arms.
When the snowmen start to drown
in themselves I tell them to stand up
straight and take it. Only idiots
are fireproof. Only the fireproof whimper
and howl. Our resolve burns us.
The coal sinks deeper into the face.
You're on fire and then you're ash,
an intriguing substance but nothing
compared to exothermic oxidation.
Dumb questions open the door to
dumb answers but dumb answers groan
and do not enter. Ash mingles,
blows in the face, a thing to breathe.
I was excited so fell asleep. A rain
dusts the hairstyle and falls to my feet
that sink into a mire. They are going
somewhere. I am not coming back.

Symptom A

1

I never have to dream again.

2

The sun seems to emerge from
behind the horn. The army of ulnas
crunches under the boulder.

3

The marigold tile wraps around the corner.

4

What is the frog looking at?

5

I have band-aids. No one is wounded.

The Cicatrix

I love the cicatrix which runs
                    like a ridge
behind your eyes. It
                    has been called sky and
you
        have been called sky
                    of light when you waltz
between the lioness
                    and the lawn chair,
reach out and clasp the empty
                    air around you.
Nonnavigable, you
                    are not sky, skin of off-white
wedding dress, green
                    light beside the mountain
range.
        Air will never fall
                    into or out of grip.
You might drive into
                    a fog or walk through
flooded streets,
                    you might drop from an invisible
ladder. Clouded lover,
                    silent idea,
even in sky you
                    are not sky, you
slip quick
        from unopened and weathered lips.

Poem

Cicadas and my love
under the juniper tree
where she like a sea horse

rocks to and fro
as if the source
of sea foam and all

the frothy flowers
that mesh together
aglow before nightfall

she rocks and rattles
window panes
during quiet evenings

when my only thought
takes shape as the burning
carcass of a hedgehog

under a black light or

as shadows rising toward
honeysuckle   so

where do the suicides go?

we have nothing to do
before dying

flap your wings
fly to me

To His Mistress Going to Bed

Take down your hair and come to bed.

The druids did not keep diaries,
but said their prayers
                    and were done with it.

The Eurasian plant droops at our feet
—a plea for rain, and somehow its leaves

already seem wet. Small and white,
the flowers spread and hover, each stem

a street of open umbrellas.
Meanwhile, night. It oozes
                    and surrounds us.

We can go rough hewing, or yodel
the abandon in your gaze, cross

the open field of your abdomen.
Must we prolong the dearth?
                    The sound of

a gallop crosses your face.

Muffle my optic nerves, smother me
in the black ski mask of your undressing.

Sparrow the blood, form the humming—

I drown in faint echoes
whose source I cannot find.

Postscript

You are the one who always
throws a sweater away—

you draw faces
on tables and expect the air
to wipe the surface clean—

you want to live
in a city and then bury yourself
in woodchips

because the porch lights
overwhelm the retina—

when I pull you
out from under the pile,
you walk across the chips

with a feather behind your ear
but you do not
spontaneously take flight.

Your head is full of
this orange air so bright

you feel that I am closer,
not the feather
falling to the ground.

Condensation

The damp light today sponges up
in the fingernails, turning sideways
always to lance
the hailstorm approaching

our sandstone town or snap elastic
the half-eaten apple
in dawn. I asked and was disgusted
to drink the colorless horizon.

Crags crawl up the shoreline.
The cast-iron cooking pot sheds rust
over the kitchen floor. As if
to have a mind of winter were to be

fist-shackled
in the frozen bucket, shackled and blue
and peeling from myself. I come down slowly
in lambskin to touch

the fractured femur, to pivot
and open the wallpaper
blue mist, for this is a morning of
numbly stuck ocean-salted faces,

silence so vast it annihilates everything.
For now I have this head
yet no metallic stethoscope.
What sort of man am I made of?

Three Days in Omaha

1

Ocean's candle, the beam
breaking through your eye.

2

The blaze of the iron.
The mold in the corner.

3

All our grapes
relaxing in the noon light.

4

The elephant statue
smiled
as I walked by.

5

Figs

6

The draft running up
my pits. The dead phone lines,
the humming, whimpering.

7

Green potatoes.
New wool.
The itchy French.
Couldn't get the mud
off the boots.

8

F, not S
then a long breath
trying not to crinkle
the plastic wrap.

9

Balloons
under the lamps
on the freeway.

Echo Train

I felt as though I were walking
but I was sitting and my feet were numb,
my ankles popped and popped.
Was that a train track running between my legs?
Whatever you were saying I wanted you
to keep saying it. I could hear nothing else
and that was like sleeping,
that was like being on a train that's so noisy
you forget you're on a noisy train
and are drowned by the sunlight
that slips between the passengers' shadows.
Was that a smudged window holding up my arm?
Whatever you were saying I wanted you
to keep saying it, to swear you'd never stop,
but you needed air, you were not a diver,
not a giant lung, and in the sudden pauses
I felt as though the train were a small dog
that had attached itself to my leg.
I wanted to help him. I had no money.
I coughed and hiccupped because
the morning was green mist.
The mist was undoing my hair
and if the shopkeepers saw me with this dog
I'd be unable to explain myself.
That's like drowning. That's like slipping
off a pier, the cracked pier, the rotting pier,
the one that's stitched with seaweed,
the one you're always pointing at
saying whatever you're saying which must
soon stop. Okay, I know it's stupid
to set up these ideals. I like to walk
behind these prop-like thoughts
and run my fingers over the surface to see
how deep the structure goes.

If the grass is wet the feet feel cold and slimy.
The birds still sing. I try not to cough.
Soon I'll be the up-and-coming moss.

Radio Station

You have to pass the dead animal smell, and the doors
get stuck, so push. We are allowed to curse, but
if one glares at any nearby object the
shadows seem to creep out the door. They call that
the oozing light. The best place to drink is at
the faucet but it is sometimes impossible to turn off
so you have to stand there and keep drinking.

The light bulbs, if we turn them on,
make rings around the microphones and you
can feel that you are speaking into some small nebula.
The glass shatters on the hour, the hour hums.
We pick the obvious things to talk about. The rabbits
in the neighbor's farm. The watermelons, will
they be small or large. What we will call
the clusters of children popping up each spring.

They tiptoe and think it's funny. They poke at each
other's eyes. They throw sand at the treetops.
They don't care about eyesight. They hide water
in sentences. They gurgle for days. They choke
on their cheeks. Their muscles get tangled up.
Their hair gets tangled up. Their arms are uncontrollable.
They are not allowed to touch the knobs.

The knobs contain a pigment that comes off
in the hands but we have soap nearby
and it only takes a minute to rub off. All the callers
must say the call number. That's the rule. People sometimes
run by the window as if trying to distract us and
make us laugh. But we are well trained.
We can look at them and show no sign of recognition.

New Farmhand

We were in the badger state
milking cows and mopping floors
and we stood up like flowers
leaning on each other to smell

fresh dirt. Each morning I felt
as though the peace lily were growing
from my tummy. Your skirt
was as though a peace lily had had

the fabric baby. I am not from here,
you whispered though you wanted
everyone to hear. The regional accents
were smothered on my face, I was

wearing umbrellas that blocked
the sun. The Cheerios stuck to the bottom
of my feet but I didn't care, I liked
the crunch, how I seemed to be crossing

a fragile galaxy and my lazy wings
weren't working. Ho hum, I hated flying,
my arms ran into the wall, the wall

creased like a dress shirt, my helmet
hardly held the window up. The wind was
an accident. Ancient, but no less
a nuisance. No one dreamt of water.

Somnambulist

1

My sleep is a locker.
My breath pushes out the laughing angel.

2

Nobody lives here.
The day bleeds red paint on the posters.

3

The day pumps hummingbirds
through the steel portals of your breath.

4

I sleep in the black curve
that cuts across the blue circle.

5

A beast snarls because my finger tips
tap lightly on the dashboard.

6

I press the yellow button.
The bag of lemons drops to the floor.

7

The hot coils cool down. I step through
the streak of green rushing by the window.

What Are You Taking to the Potluck?

I hope it rains.
The Styrofoam plates jut out like
a new beach. Wish I could see that on tape.
I can hear a little voice pulsing,
honest. What color are new beets? I'll give
away whatever, lemon-water, that little
jug. I don't know where it came from.
When the light hits it right it's like a volcano.
Why do I suddenly feel so sentient?
In the bird, the flower.
In the flower, the thumb. Something
churrs anyway. It's like running but
I see no need to move. The strings stiffen,
the maps unfold and rip. It's like sleeping.
You want to hang on.
Your hands unfold and slip.

Anonymous Master

The monk was praying. We were not surprised
but wished he'd quit. It was time to eat.
His elbows were blocking the platter and the
bulbs could not sprout for what seemed like
several summers strewn with intermittent showers, warm fronts,
occasional cold bouts. It was like
laundry day all over again. I could smell the soap, felt
the wet rags between my hands. I was pretending to make comments
to the earwig on the couch in the corner.
Fucking A. Those light beams came screaming out of the shadow.
I wanted to know if you knew. Nobody nodded.

House Party

1

Tea leaves line the walkways and from the rafters
hang several cloves of garlic. The afternoons accumulate
like extra thumbs. Night comes in quick
and leaps over the park so we call it the glove.
If the glove gets in the laundry we have to let it air dry.

2

Some of the birds never go to sleep and
are frightened to have to watch the moon.
They feel lost in the glove that rubs between their feathers.
They feel alone as they look at each other's beaks.
I leave the lights on for them.

3

Sunshine is the common form of address.
Sunshine amputates the lily patch,
gets stuck in the fronds. Sunshine leaves the lights on.
That's what we say to say we are hungry.

4

Here's the tool shed filled with armchairs.
Here's the pond we have to re-dig each summer.
We are satisfied if fish are swimming. We say: sunshine, are
you sleepy? The sleepers sleep in. I stand beside
to help them snore. They do not wake up. I feel dirty and golden.
I never wash.

5

The kingbird throws itself at the water to bathe.
The kingbird is my friend so we don't have to speak.
He nods and it's time for a bath. I'm always bathing.
The kingbird sits above me and eats his insects.
It's like a diner out here, I say. He does not respond.
We don't like each other too much. My arms grow sore.
The glove tugs on me. I can't whistle until dawn.

The Helping Hand
for Leat Klingman

They must be humble, these headless birds
that line the walk. They help me with my math
homework. They whisper, they whistle, they say
my shoes stink. I tell Mom I like sandals better.
The birds say I should find a volcano
but they promise not to throw me in.
They say they'll teach me how to swim, and I
buy trunks and a red beach towel and wait
for them at the city pool. When the weather's nice
they help out with the road work. They peck
at our towers and make us pick up the pieces
and place them in a jar. We write a number
on each jar. We make a wall of jars.
The birds are alarmed by the giraffe
and annoyed by the graffiti. They cannot read.
Instead, they eat. They sleep with our widows.
They shriek when we listen and coo when they're alone.
They hate our windows and try to break them
with their hardhats. I want to wear such hardhats
but have no work to do. They say go home and wash
your hands. They pet us with their wings.
The wings are shaped like eyebrows. Their eyebrows
burn in water. The water is their home.
They can close their eyes because they do not have them.

Coda

Headless bird, where are you going?
Birdless head, what are you saying?
Treeless sky, what are you growing?
Skyless bird, what are you thinking?

Landscape

These shoestrings are very beautiful when
they are not tied around my neck and
if I wrap them around my forearm it's like we're
looking at a farm or window or giant lake

of windows whose ripples never quite resemble
the skin. It is dry and just sits there as though
an irrigation plant had not been turned on
so now the truckers have nothing to take to us,

but we never liked what they took us anyhow.
The thought of roads that went on forever.
We liked that. And how the shadows of
the trucks were like black boxes that moved

so quickly they were not rattled by the bumps
and pebbles and rises in the road. The blood
does not make the skin quake. The air runs in
and around. Picks up kite, sets it down.

Another Posture

The sense of the body flowing from an old comfortable posture
to a new, exciting yet strange position
will dominate the first short steps of the foray into the next leg
of the never-ending day trip. But after a few hours

of non-aggravated nods and smiles,
a new batch of less convenient messages comes streaming
out the windows in streaks of red and blue.
They sizzle as they are moved by something like a cue ball

through the humid air that seeps inside the skin
and helps our clothes come off. For once in the history
of automobiles the motorists do not stop to gawk
but keep plodding merrily toward their destinations

of various consequences, fruit stands, motel parking lots,
mirror factories. Perhaps they already know
that the longer lens only puts different elements out of focus.
The center point of the picture is impossible to identify,

and one can easily forget it is a picture in the first place.
The brush and bushes get in the way. We spend too much time
tracing their shadows as they sway back and forth
in the late afternoon breeze. Yes, it *is* a good environment for a nap.

Even the occasional outside voice does not bother our sleep
that is not exactly sleep but a notch or two below wakefulness
so that if desired we could catalogue and name all
that goes on around us. The sunlight alternating between pure

and cloud-masked. The birds beginning their evening calls.
Sounds that coagulate like blood around a day-old puncture wound,
and bouquets — the mint lip-balm and vanilla candle
stirring together in the breeze that in a few weeks will be ushering
      away the leaves.

With this premonition I feel suddenly dropped
in an insipid body of water that barely flows toward a towering mass
of rock and sand. No, those aren't cliff swallows floating overhead.
A dog barks, the barge that is the body gurgles and moves on.

Book of Clouds

The window curtain flutters
through the long hallways
and creeps
under the eyelids of the boy

dreaming of his glass hammer
which vanished after he placed it
in the cupboard
and went to the lavatory

to wash his face. So we too
must be placed
in the cupboard and vanish.
Our seats are seeping

earthward
and the sky swoops down
to infiltrate our files and data books.
At least we can seize

the outlines and rust-shaded
impressions
of tress and birds as they expand
with each minute

of the afternoon.
Soon they will form
an awning that will cover us
from the sun

and the terrible openness
in which my baldhead shimmers
like a fleet
of cabs of a rainy night.

~

No I don't really know
what to do
with the things of which
I speak to you—

frosted mug, candle, eucalyptus,
whatever tries to eat it,
whatever drapes across my lap,
whatever climbs the wall.

No I do not believe
in eyes. And
I have no idea why
the tapering outline of an owl

crosses your face
as it pulls me forward into
some secret stop
between bus stops.

~

The hairclip is lost in the oversized pocket
and the absolute
focus of one lens on another
ruins

the freshness of the experiment.
Like a camera
that photographs
itself in a mirror,

the road
envelops the destination
we are driving into,
but the revised dictionary

needs neither our pictures
nor the tales
of where we have been
with our forks

and knives
and poor knowledge
of the local language and customs.
The book is open and simple,

like the teeth you spent
so long cleaning.
The creased paper
barely gleams.

      ~

And like the melody of a mass in b-minor
your *you* paces
alongside its counter-point
all day. The lily blossoms, the room

stands still.
Your *you* drives across
my chest,
crawls toward the air filter.

Toward this center
of gravity, the center of song,
this question
I had been forming without

looking in the other basement,
the one with the watermarks,
the one that's almost white
except that the light is not

allowed to enter.
Well, in that semi-sacred cavity
I impersonate the drawings
gathered around the first chord

and ensuing bonfire of syllabic frost,
and from that
fresh area of wherever,
a dauntingly large wire emerges

to emit the signals
I constantly confuse
with heat, earrings, the heart's half-
opened valves, myself, a cluster

of foam figurines. The
gelatinous phantoms carry
the feather-light purses
and half-read books away.

Foghorn

The white bunny leaps from my palms.
The magic marker breaks in my pocket.
Sometimes I feel like slicing a line
in the skin of my scalp. Sometimes
I look at the clouds and feel nauseous.
I have to attend this meeting that
will be like trying to fall asleep with
a headache. Sometimes I have to open
a door just to remember I'm in a room.
And I have this dream where I'm camping
next to a glacier but I can't feel my toes,
in fact, they've disappeared and have
been replaced by nylon stuff bags
which are ripped and shrinking.
When the circus is in town I do not go.
The gravel parking lot becomes a mess.
The motors churn and the rotors fling
small greasy pieces in all directions. Gradually
the wall beside my bed gets higher.
At the top an archer walks back and forth
basking in the sun. In the last hours
of the afternoon he falls asleep but I
do not invite him to my bed. He must
lie down by the willow that shades the moat.
Why do I live in this castle a million miles
from the action? The balloons are popping
but I cannot feel them. I am a giant toothache.

Am I a Deck of Cards?

I wonder as I drive behind the truck
whose load of leaves is blowing
all over the windshield and making me
also wonder if I will have to bear with
this decomposing blizzard for the rest of
the ride through the ruddy half-lit streets.
As if in protest I steer with my pinky
and with my other hand rub at the chalk
on my pants. Some of the radio songs
are composed of nothing but answers.
Some of the answers pierce us in two places
like a staple passing through the flesh,
though they hold nothing together.
Everything they touch drifts apart.
Everything they touch becomes a swarm
of dying bees. The sky dissects them
so that they may again be beautiful.
We buzz by the carcass of a mourning dove
and do not stop because we are growing
like geraniums and have no time to lose
though time is never gained or lost.
You think you can sift through it, collect it
and count it out and count on it like a binding
substance used in carpentry. My house is
always teetering. It cracks and groans
and may soon be scattered splints of wood.
The sky holds nothing to the ground.

Surface Cloud

1

The sky fills with departing geese.

2

Fire leaps from the blood.

3

The body made of water wallows in the shadows.

4

Sun strikes the forehead.

5

Silky pavement runs in all directions.

Easy Listening

A blue jay perches on the railing
and the cuff of my shirt is brighter
than the sky so I wasn't listening
to the instructions. I can hear
a heartbeat and the tapping of
a spoon. I think my brain is a spool
of thread. You can see it in my forehead.
When you pull on one end,
the other end shivers. The dark
sky shatters. Clouds accumulate
and disperse. Again the dust settles.
Again the chimes fall silent. Are
you listening to the instructions?
To the west I thought I saw a diamond.
Turned out to be nothing but air.
Once I ate a square of butter because
I thought it was cheese. The willows
lilt and rustle. I love their hairstyle
just as I love your salty skin. The
napkin falls to the floor. The instructions
brush past the face. After whispering
for an hour it is natural to feel tired.
The mud is speckled with green dots.
I won't be jumping in that pond.
The sky ripples and is gone. I wasn't
listening. I have an oboe in my hand.

Aroma Therapy

Your entrance is never a segue.
Your beauty is a bouquet of fossils.
The marks on your hand
are the marks on my hand.
Your surface is always reloading.
Your caravan is never exploding.
When I have an idea, you are
spilling coffee in it. You are wearing
yellow and standing by the pink door.
Your moth wings are wheels rolling
on a floor of cinder blocks.
My arms flailing, my teeth gnashing.
Your mirror is the swarm of locusts
thrashing through the office window.
Your mirror is that watermelon
sliced and sweating on the sidewalk.
Your flecks are the plumes of paper factories.
I live in the shadow of your stage coach.
I sleep in the corner of your ice castle.
Luminescence breeds in our despair.

Inside Out

1

I felt a farm growing beneath my nose
and every honking horn
was a flower about to bloom,
a river was about to crest.

2

Water crashed into the sheds and ditches,
sky squeezed into a nutshell
and all the sweaters turned to thread
—spools of thread floating in the sky.

3

A shadow overtook the marigolds
and for a time it seemed as though
these things would just keep happening
under the open sky's swishing and gurgling.

4

Was I a field of roots and sparrows?
Was I the fold, the soil, the furrow?
When the telephone rang I refused to answer.

5

Fresh caterpillars slouched and withered.
The candlelight inside my mouth
shrunk to the size of a fingernail.
Humph.
        —New sky, old sky, same sky.

6

In the candle, the sky.
In the dirt, the road.
In the mouth, an answer—

a shadow, a river, my shadow—

Vanishing Point

In the shadow
the darting beetles.

~

Near the door
the nervous pacing.

~

Sometimes when I'm waiting
I'm just breathing.

~

Hazy mountain,
moonlight on the stream.

~

The ocean and the sandbar
and the lines the tide makes.

~

Looking through the window
suddenly embarrassed.

~

Here is the wall,
something to lean against.

~

The dunes sloping,
the seagulls making figure-eights.

∾

A dark shape moves
beneath a boulder.

∾

Listening,
I shine the light into the cupboard.

Hanging the Whale

I am affixing the little whale to the wall.
Ugly wall, ugly whale, ugly hand reaching out
like something in the mind that turns
toward these webs and screens and
absorbs their bloated gamma rays. Whatever

girds girds me well — I feel encircled by
a mountain range that closes over me.
The peaks clasp together, the sky disappears.
A machine is beeping and the little whale
dives into my arms and squeezes me into

myself so I am a small body of water
in a shrinking porous container. A granite
slab of facial expressions rises like the mist
of a pond in the morning. At last I have
found an island in which there is not a single

random occurrence. No dancing bees,
no mumbling bushes of fire bolted
to the walkways. Only a box that will not
open, straight ears of corn, a sky of twilight
cumulous. The whale holds the wall together

and the air moistens. Minutes before
the storm the hair my neighbor grows
tumbles in the breeze and takes the rest
of her head with it. The whale holds together.
The whole street breathes.

The Sam Plan

My telephone is an elephant
named Sam who keeps his eyes closed
unless I touch the number pad
or speak clearly into the receiver.

Sam, I say, I am tired of talking only to you.
Sam rubs my shoulders with his trunk.
Sam, I ask, what do you think
of Elizabethan optical theory? I love

the idea that light comes from our eyes.
Sam shrugs and begins fiddling
with a gadget I have never seen before.
Is it a tourniquet? I hope not,

for the tourniquet would require
an open vein to stop from bleeding.
Sam, I say, I am tired of looking at my door
expecting it to open or burst into flames.

Now that I have drunk all the water
I will turn off the lights one by one.
I will plug the phone into the outlet.
Sam is not its real name.

Burrito

The baby is in the blanket.
The toes are on the bed.
The finger is in the socket.

The ego is in the pocket.
The pasture is in the mind.
The hammer is in the tool box.

The cloud is in the mouth.
The fortress is on the foothills.
The fens are to the south.

The matches are in the fire.
The fire is up the wall.
The error is in the wires.

The gadget is on the shelf.
The shelf is over the shelf.

The self is in the doorway.
The lights are all around.

The plants are in the ground.
The ground is in the sky.
The ground is in the ground.

Mouth of Clouds

When I wake up the fish quit swimming.
The windows rattle, the rain drips.
The color orange is in my hand but
when I wake up the rhododendron
wavers, its shadow creeps across
the corrugated cardboard and I can't stop
thinking about the black pebbles,
their sheen under the running stream.
When I wake up the sailors are tired
of sailing. When I wake up they are bathing
on the hot rocks. They are each
growing the same beard. When I wake up
I have an idea. I hang my keys
on the hook and take off my shoes.
I fall back to sleep. I put the banana
in my cereal. I offer a prayer to the highway.
When I wake up I am a transparent eyeball.
When I wake up the telephone makes
a boiling sound. The walls hiss. The windows
shiver and frost over. The waitstaff cringes
because when I wake up I'm here to stay.
I take my breath and blow it in the sawdust.

Wool

The sheep bow their heads
because they must go away
indefinitely. They are tired
of the sky resting on their backs.

When we stand up, the sheep
do not raise their heads.
They want to become the grass.
Threshers keep time with the breeze.

I do not bow my head.
The bark peels off in my hands.
My hands loop around each other,
the sky comes back indefinitely.

The breeze blows the leaves
in the direction of the light.
I thought a cloud waved hello.
The sky flashed its ozone shirt.

If the crows stopped shaking
their heads—if the cow's eye
met my eye—up the hill we'd be
a uniform stitched by the sun.

The sheep can breathe.
The sheep cannot breathe.
The sheep and the sky—
the sky, the mist, the breeze.

Footprints

I had a nice fern.
Now I paste the paper to the cardboard.

I often drank water with my head out the window.
Now the color green soaks into my bones.

~

Interesting story:
the bananas floating
down the river.

~

Hens come up the sidewalk.
They are not looking for anyone in particular.

~

I had a neon sign.
Now what? Now what?

I had a minute left.
I offered the lip balm to the meter maid.

~

The rhododendron beside the stoop
is losing its flowers.

~

Funny story:
The magic marker
crushed under my feet.

~

I had a headache as I walked across the farm.
The moon would not stop glowing.

Delete That

The series of numbers
and letters
has a way of numbing
the eyes and overhauling the yellow

and green and orange
images on the wall.
I'd delete everything
and open the door

and smell the grass.
The pixilated iguana
pushes back but does not
snarl, never snarls.

On the top of the hill
a patch of sunlight
and my foot.
On the other side

of the wall, the street
seems to slither. I'd never
delete the damp pavement.
When I find grass

in my lip
I am not about to jot
down a note. *I am hungry.*
Are you the crumb

in my pocket?
The architect coughs
toward the empty
lot. The hopping robin

erases his prints.

The Wrong Side of Waking

The earrings sparkle
before the arrival of dusk.

The mind swims backwards
shivering
in the narcoleptic breeze.

Every grimace blossoms
and deteriorates.

Day of Capes

I remember the sneeze in the pouring rain.

The man said the cloud was a steel water bottle.

Bottle of firmament. Bottle of ice and daylight.

When the woman walked past the corner the street turned
red, then reddish green, and the thunder hurried us under the
awning.

The man gnawed on his paper airplane.

A cat peeked through the flower.

Flower window. Ice and bottles.

When the window came to pieces in our fingers we were only
 children, leaning on each other's skin.

Holding Patterns

I was a floating horse and in my folded hand
I was floating without eyes or ears.
I was floating when the rain came
and I was floating when the flood came
and when everyone died.

~

So I folded up my hand
and I lived in the old travel chest.
And I lived in a pouch of tobacco.
And I lived in a cavern in a hill.

~

When it was summer everyone was talking
and singing, walking and stopping, rising and falling.
Some sediment floated through the air.
Some sediment landed on my arms
and on my collar bone and on my head
and I began to feel untied from the earth
even as the earth tried to claim me as its own.
The sky, too, zipped through my ears.

~

In another song I mourned the loss of friends.
They weren't dead, just preoccupied.
I was a floating horse and in my folded hand
I carried their poems and pictures.

~

I was holding a kite and living deep beneath my head.
The string was looped around my pinkie, then my thumb.
A woman carried me iced-coffees every day
and the sweater I was knitting would never be finished

~

because the body kept growing,
because the leaves were blowing away,
because I was a floating horse,
because I was living in my hand,
because the thread was made of a sand,
because I was knitting flames folded in flames.

~

A small red ball bounced over the staircase
which I could not walk up because
I was living beneath it in a suitcase
and painting realistic pictures of the staircase,
and I hated the staircase and the painting
became a lion whose mane was a flame,
a flame about to burn the staircase down.

~

But you were so nice when I lived
in your armchair. It was as though a train
were coming straight for us every day
but would never arrive.

~

It was good that our bodies were not sliced in half.
It was good to be together even as we were apart.
We could eat clementines and roll the seeds
between our tongues and teeth which were
musical notes floating in the breeze.

～

Now that I am a whistle everything blows through me.
I live in a city where every day my jeans are new,
orange paper lines the streets, green leaves of light
pierce through the windows, and the windows flex
and open onto oceans. The oceans hold us back
until the waves crest and break and free us.
Our elbows flap and bend, and I am happy
because they hold the hands up and keep us afloat
and we do not think twice before breathing.

Scrapbook

If my brow did not brown
under the sun. If my headband

were a tuft of blond hair.
If the surf crept up the shoreline

and massaged my scalp.
If my finger steadied itself

on the edge of the shard.
If the day I woke up

I woke up. If I turned
from sky to flesh and sunk

into sunlit blood.
If I felt the yellow shirt drifting

off my body, my body lost in a draft,
my body becoming the next draft.